R[illegible] nd the
CHOC[illegible]S GANG

DRAGON
GRAFTON BOOKS
A Division of the Collins Publishing Group

LONDON GLASGOW
TORONTO SYDNEY AUCKLAND

RUPERT is buying Easter eggs in the sweet shop at Nutwood when his pal, Bill Badger, storms in.

'Look at this,' he exclaims, holding up a bag of chocolate buttons.

'I see you've eaten most of them already,' Rupert grins.

'That's the point – I HAVEN'T!' says Bill angrily. 'I opened this packet a moment ago, and what do I find? Just THREE buttons inside.'

The shopkeeper looks upset. 'I don't understand it,' he mutters. 'That's the third one like that this morning.'

'Perhaps something went wrong at the chocolate factory,' suggests Rupert.

The shopkeeper shakes his head. 'There's more to it than that,' he says.

He points to a jar of chocolate buttons on the shelf behind. 'That was nearly full last night. Nobody has come in to buy any – but now it's almost empty!'

'Somebody must have stolen them,' cries Rupert.

'I suppose so,' says the shopkeeper doubtfully. 'But nothing else is missing. And every BAG of buttons is sealed – so how do you get them out without tearing the packets?'

He gives a puzzled frown, and weighs out some more buttons for Bill.

'I don't understand it and that's a fact,' he sighs.

On their way home, Bill looks thoughtful. 'Perhaps I should buy some more before they ALL disappear,' he says.

But it is early closing day in Nutwood, and the sweet shop is shut when they go back.

Rupert glances through the window – and then stares in surprise.

Four tiny masked figures are hard at work loading chocolate buttons into little sacks!

'Who are they?' cries Bill.

'Nutwood Gnomes!' gasps Rupert. 'Come on – let's try to catch them.'

At the sound of their voices the robbers drop their bags in panic and rush out through the back door. 'After them,' shouts Rupert.

But by the time the chums reach the back alley, the little figures have escaped.

'We must see the Chief Gnome about this,' says Rupert grimly.

The Nutwood Gnomes live under Nutwood Common, and Rupert and the Chief Gnome are old friends.

'It sounds like Nipper Gnome and his gang,' exclaims the Chief Gnome when Rupert tells him what has happened. 'The Gnome Squad has been after them for some time.'

'But why are they stealing chocolate buttons?' asks Rupert.

'I'll show you,' says the Chief Gnome, unlocking a large cupboard.

Inside are rows of Easter eggs!

The Chief Gnome gives Rupert and Bill one each. 'What do you think to these?' he demands.

'They look all right to me,' grins Bill.

'Exactly!' cries the Chief Gnome. 'They LOOK right and they TASTE right but they're NOT right – they're fakes!'

'Fakes?' gulps Rupert.

The Chief Gnome slams the cupboard door shut. 'Made by Nipper Gnome out of melted down chocolate buttons,' he declares angrily.

He turns to the chums. 'Nipper must have a secret factory somewhere. Have you any idea where it could be?'

'I'm afraid we didn't see which way the gang went,' says Bill regretfully.

But Rupert has an idea. 'I noticed some buttons on the Common as we came along,' he exclaims. 'The robbers must have dropped them. Perhaps there is a trail we can follow.'

The Chief leaps to his feet. 'I'll get the Gnome Police on to this immediately,' he cries.

Gnome policemen with large magnifying glasses are soon searching the spot that Rupert points out.

One of them gives an excited shout – he has found a trail of buttons in the grass.

They lead into a field bordering the Common. Rupert notices a tiny barn there, half-hidden by bushes and weeds.

'That must be Nipper's hideout,' whispers the Gnome Inspector.

The gang are taken completely by surprise when the police burst in.

There are heaps of buttons everywhere – and a neat stack of tiny Easter eggs by a cauldron of hot chocolate.

Rupert spots something else too – little cutters for opening packets of chocolate buttons, and a blowlamp for sealing up the bags again.

'You're all under arrest,' shouts the Inspector, snapping handcuffs on Nipper Gnome.

The Chief Gnome is delighted. He tells Rupert that Nipper and his gang will all go behind bars – not the chocolate sort but the real thing.

Then he gives the chums the stolen chocolate to take back to the sweetshop. 'We are sorry that most of the buttons are now eggs,' he says.

But the shopkeeper doesn't mind a bit. 'People prefer eggs at Easter,' he smiles.

And he thanks Rupert and Bill by giving them – yes, you guessed it – A LARGE EASTER EGG EACH!

Dragon
Grafton Books
A Division of the Collins Publishing Group
8 Grafton Street, London W1X 3LA

Published by Dragon Books 1986

Written by Len Collis
Illustrated by Jon Davis
Designed by Ralph Semmence

ISBN 0 583 31056 7

Printed by Ancient House Press, Ipswich, Suffolk

Set in Palatino